The Eight Life Lessons

Timeless Wisdom for Modern Living

JERAMY ROBERTS

The Eight Life Lessons: Timeless Wisdom for
Modern Living

Published by Sustained Concepts Inc.

450 Central Way, Kirkland WA.

Copyright © 2024 Jeramy Roberts

For permissions contact: JeramyRoberts@gmail.com

Paperback:
ISBN: 979-8-9917192-0-9

Digital Online:
ISBN: 979-8-9917192-1-6

Dedications

*Kathleen for telling me what I didn't want to
hear, when we both knew I couldn't hear it.
My grandmother, who imparted to me
a true sense of class and style.
Auntie Kelly The beacon of light,
overshadowed by nothing else.
My Mother who did the best she could even if she couldn't.
My Dad that taught me what it was to walk the earth.*

CONTENTS

Introduction. vii

Chapter 1. Reacting Emotionally 1

Chapter 2. The Only Certainty 9

Chapter 3. Selfish-ish. 17

Chapter 4. You Attract What You Are 25

Chapter 5. The Way You Do One Thing 33

Chapter 6. Core Values 41

Chapter 7. The map & The Territory 49

Chapter 8. The World Is a Mirror 59

INTRODUCTION

I wrote this book to be simple and direct. Each chapter explains a lesson that I have learned, with a very easy but no less effective tip or single step that anyone can use to implement the lesson in their own life. Always remember: the simplest path is almost always the most effective and profound. This is by no means a comprehensive guide to life; rather, it is a place of fundamental understanding, a baseline, as it were. I still focus on these tenets personally and come back to them often, as they are important regardless of how far along you perceive yourself to be in the journey of growth.

Similarly, it is worth mentioning that these are what I consider to be the most important and fundamental lessons on the journey of self-discovery, on the road to each of our hopes, goals, and dreams. Regardless of class, race, religion, or gender identity, these lessons are universal and have held true for thousands of years. Each lesson was hard-earned and pulled from multiple sources over a considerable amount of time, through effort, hope, pain, and even, at times, despair. I came across them out of necessity, the necessity that drove the will to create a better life for myself or, at the very least, to feel a real sense of accomplishment at the end of it all.

The single step or tip I describe to implement each lesson is of my own design, born of that same necessity, the need to have something simple to grasp onto long enough for a new way to take hold. In the maelstrom of struggle, I hardly had the wherewithal to contemplate these things, let alone follow a concise and lengthy checklist or routine of growth. There was a time when all I knew was that I needed to find a way to do better.

Oftentimes, as I wrote the following pages, I would chuckle at myself and wish I could have had this book all those years ago. This thought, of course, is folly; the struggle and desperation molded me into the person I am proud of today, and I would trade it for nothing. I hope my mistakes, struggles, and desperations serve you as well as they have served me. If they do not, that, of course, will serve you just as well.

REACTING EMOTIONALLY

"We often drown not because we fall into a river, but because we stay submerged in it." – *Paulo Coelho*

The first step to personal growth is to stop reacting emotionally. This is something I emphasize with every student or colleague who comes to me for help, and it's the same principle that guided the start of my own journey over 20 years ago. Controlling your emotional reactions is key because, until you do, you're unable to truly see the reality of the situations you're facing or decide how you want to respond.

Most of us have a knee-jerk reaction to things happening around us. Take a simple scenario, someone cuts in front of you in line. The typical response is immediate irritation, and often, words are spoken before we've even had a chance to fully register the situation. But this is exactly what we need to change. Instead of reacting impulsively, we must pause and think. What's actually happening here? How do I want to respond?

By gaining control over how we react, we begin to see situations more clearly. This shift affects everything, from the opportunities that come our way to the relationships we attract into our lives, even our character as a whole. Most importantly, it shapes our overall perception of the world, and in the end, perception is all we have.

Often, when someone says or does something negative, it has little to do with us and more to do with what's going on in their life. They could be stressed, insecure, or just having a bad day. And even if it is directed at you, handling it without emotional control only fuels more negativity. When you learn to manage your emotional reactions, you'll not only begin to see where others are coming from but also develop the ability to respond in a way that aligns with who you want to be.

Over time, this awareness will extend to recognizing when others are being genuine or when they're acting out of fear or insecurity. Many people are unknowingly deceiving themselves and others because their perception of reality is skewed. They don't mean to, they are simply not seeing things clearly.

Learning to manage emotional responses is crucial because adversity is a constant in life. Daily encounters with negativity are inevitable, but the way we handle these moments determines the quality of our experiences. Adversity doesn't always stem from ill intent; it's often a byproduct of the human condition. People are busy, stressed, and focused on their own lives, and this can lead to friction. That's why it's so important to take a moment to stop, breathe, and think about how you want to react.

As you practice this, emotional control will become your default mode. Eventually, you'll find yourself remaining calm in situations that used to trigger you. When someone cuts in front of you in line or says something unkind, instead of reacting impulsively, you'll pause, consider the situation, and decide how to respond. This space for reflection gives you the opportunity to understand where the other person is coming from. Are they stressed? Is their action directed at you, or are they just having a bad day?

Most negativity isn't personal. It's rarely directed at you with malicious intent; it's just life being hard for everyone. Many people pass their stress onto others, but when you break this cycle, you free up energy, energy you can use to focus on who you want to become.

By controlling your emotional responses, you'll start to embody the traits you admire in others. You'll stop replaying conversations in your head, wishing you'd handled them differently. You'll become the person who says the right things in the moment, not mentally replaying the conversation to yourself hours later. This self-awareness is the gateway to growth.

One simple technique to start practicing emotional control is to fake a smile and take a breath. I know it sounds silly, but trust me, it works. Smiling, even when it feels forced, triggers a physiological response in your body. It takes effort at first, but in negative situations, this small act can shift your emotional state almost immediately.

Try it in your car during stressful traffic or at the grocery store when someone's being rude. At first, it will feel awkward because the smile isn't genuine. But with practice, it will become second nature, and eventually, the smile will reach your eyes. This technique interrupts your automatic emotional reactions, allowing you a moment to think before responding.

As you keep practicing, you'll start noticing shifts in how you perceive and handle situations. You'll see that most people are, in fact, stressed or afraid, and often, their actions have nothing to do with you. This realization brings a sense of calm, and you'll notice that you too have room for improvement in how you respond to others.

Recognizing your own shortcomings is a powerful point of growth. It's when you realize, "Hey, I can change how I handle things," that real progress begins. Your subconscious mind will help you shift toward being the calm, composed person you want to be.

Over time, these new habits will become part of your character. You'll begin to embody the qualities of someone who is in control, and this will happen naturally as you start thinking critically in the moment. With repetition, your emotional control will become automatic.

One of the simplest ways to begin is by practicing that fake smile and a deep breath when it is not critical, when there is no stress attached to the moment, any interaction will do for a practice session. It may sound simple, but it's a foundational step toward mastering your emotions. After a while, the smile won't be fake anymore, it will come naturally, and with it, a sense of calm.

As this calmness becomes part of your nature, you'll see a ripple effect in your life. People will recognize your composure, and often, their own negativity will dissipate when faced with your calm demeanor. Negativity feeds on reaction, and when you don't give it that energy, it tends to stop in its tracks.

So, dear reader, here is your simple action plan: fake smile, breathe, and think. You don't need a checklist or elaborate exercises, just start paying attention. In moments of stress or challenge, smile, breathe, and take a moment to reflect. This small pause will eventually become second nature, transforming how you respond to the world.

THE ONLY CERTAINTY

"Art is a lie that makes us realize truth." – *Pablo Picasso*

The only certainty in life is that there is no certainty. As soon as you grasp this paradox, you'll begin to feel more secure, more at ease with the unpredictability of life. This idea may sound contradictory, but it's a powerful truth, the only real security is knowing that there is no security.

On the surface, it might seem unsettling, even counterintuitive, to accept that nothing is guaranteed. Doesn't life require careful planning and preparation? Absolutely. You can, and should, steer your life in the direction you want it to go. But here's the catch, while you can plan, you must also recognize that life's unpredictability is inevitable. That's the part most people overlook, the understanding that, despite all your planning, there is no certainty.

Let's look at it in the simplest way. You might head out for the grocery store later today, fully expecting to return home. But there's no guarantee that you'll make it back. It's a sobering thought, but it's also reality. Nothing in life is promised. Acknowledging this isn't defeatist, it's liberating. Once you understand that uncertainty is a constant, you can approach life with greater clarity and purpose.

The second part of this idea is that most people are constantly resisting change. And the way many people resist change is by trying to control everything around them. While it's natural to want some control over your life, if you hold too tightly to your plans, you risk missing out on opportunities or being unable to cope when life inevitably throws you a curveball.

The world we live in is dynamic, always in flux. Nature itself is a great teacher of this truth. Walk through a forest, and you'll see that everything is in a constant state of change, trees grow and die, seasons shift, the weather changes unpredictably. But nature doesn't resist this, it flows with the changes. And that's the lesson, the world is always moving, and so should we.

I love autumn, and not just because of the beauty of the season, but because it's a reminder of life's natural cycles. Autumn is about death, leaves fall, plants wither. Yet, it's breathtaking. That's because there's peace in accepting the inevitability of change. This perspective helps me feel more grounded when things in my own life begin to shift.

We all know, deep down, that life will bring change. Whether we want to admit it or not, something will happen to us, good or bad. The passing of time alone ensures that life will shift. Embracing this fact is the first step toward making better plans, better preparations, and having a clearer sense of direction.

When you keep this understanding in mind, your life will feel more stable. You'll be more prepared for the unexpected, and you'll see changes coming that you might otherwise have missed. This doesn't mean you'll know exactly what's around the corner, but you'll be better positioned to respond when it comes.

Perception plays a huge role in how we handle uncertainty. Many people are stuck because they can't see the opportunities that change brings. They cling so tightly to their plans and their sense of security that they become blind to the possibilities that exist beyond them. This is especially true as people get older, many build walls of certainty around themselves, and when change comes, they can't cope. They shut down because they've built their lives around the illusion that things won't change.

When life gets tough, when everything seems to be falling apart, it's this very understanding, the certainty of uncertainty that can give you the clarity to see opportunities hidden in the chaos. When you know that change is inevitable, you stop resisting it, and in that acceptance, you find power. You gain the ability to pivot, to steer your life in new directions, even in difficult times.

This shift in perception is simple but profound. While it's easy to grasp intellectually, it can be harder to fully embrace emotionally. Accepting that we're not in complete control of our lives is frightening for many people. But here's the good news, it doesn't have to be scary. In fact, once you make peace with it, life becomes much easier.

No matter how much power, money, or status you have, change will come. By accepting this, your plans and preparations become more effective. You'll be more flexible, more able to adapt, and you'll feel a deeper sense of security, not because you can control everything, but because you understand that you don't have to.

Missing out on opportunities because of a rigid attachment to security is one of the greatest tragedies of life. Fear of the unknown can cause us to hold onto what's familiar, even when something far better is waiting for us. The truth is, none of us can truly count on anything.

Once you internalize this contradiction, you'll approach situations with a fresh perspective, and that shift will bring a sense of ease. Even in moments that used to cause you anxiety, you'll feel more comfortable. Knowing that uncertainty is the only certainty, reduces fear because you stop expecting things to remain the same.

Embracing this idea is simple, so simple, in fact, that it might make you chuckle. All you need to do is think about it. That's it. Just reflect on the fact that nothing is certain, that life is always changing. Do this every day, or even just every other day, and over time, it will become part of your mindset.

There's no need for checklists, meditations, or complicated steps. Just allow yourself to consider this idea regularly. After a few weeks, you'll notice subtle shifts. You'll feel more secure, more grounded. You'll recognize that your plans, while important, can always adapt. You'll begin to see the balance between planning and embracing the unknown.

With this shift in perspective, you'll start to feel more comfortable with the fact that you can't control everything. This understanding will make you feel more secure. You'll be more confident, more at ease in your own life, and it won't be because life is predictable, it'll be because you've accepted that it isn't.

The benefits of this mindset are tremendous. You'll find yourself better prepared for whatever comes your way, and life's inevitable changes will feel less like disruptions and more like opportunities. It's a subtle shift, but it's one that will transform how you navigate the world. All it takes is a little thought, a little contemplation, and soon, you'll feel more secure than ever before.

SELFISH-ISH

"The world will ask you who you are, and if you do not know, the world will tell you." – *Carl Jung*

You can never give anyone more than you've given yourself. If you want to better yourself, help others, or do both, you must start by focusing on your own growth. It's one of those paradoxes of life, in order to give to others, you have to first give to yourself. I call this being "selfish-ish." It's not about being selfish in the negative sense, but about understanding that true growth, whether for yourself or to help others, begins with self-care and self-improvement.

There are those who strive to help others, those who focus on bettering themselves, and those who want to do both. The secret is, they're all working toward the same goal. The motivations and processes are identical. Whether you want to contribute to the world around you or make personal strides, the foundation is the same, you must look inward first. Once you grasp this, you'll make huge progress, no matter which motivation resonates with you.

This was something I learned later in my own journey of personal growth. And once I did, my entire outlook shifted, and so did my life. The goal is to become a beacon, a source of light for yourself and others. You want to embody the growth you wish to see, both in yourself and in the world. Even the smallest changes in your mindset or habits can have a ripple effect, influencing both you and those around you, often in ways that go unnoticed.

Helping yourself first isn't selfish, it's intentional growth. Whether your aim is to help others or to elevate yourself, the best way to contribute to this world is to focus on your own development. The more intentional you are about this, the more meaningful your life will become and more you will be contributing to the world in a positive way.

A lot of us are surrounded by noise, commitments, distractions and obligations that don't serve us. We say "yes" to things that fill up our time but don't really support our growth. From the moment you wake up until you go to bed, ask yourself, "Is this serving me? Is this helping me grow?" This doesn't mean cutting everyone off or saying no to everything, but it does mean being more selective about what you say "yes" to and why.

The truth is, until you give yourself the space to grow, you won't be able to fully give to others either. And here's something even deeper, the people around you, the ones who look up to you or depend on you won't be able to attain the same level of growth unless you model it first. The people you surround yourself with have a profound impact on your life. So be mindful, are your commitments, your friends, your conversations contributing to your growth, or are they just habits you've kept out of obligation or guilt?

Cutting out what doesn't serve you isn't always easy, especially if you have responsibilities like a marriage or children. But no matter your circumstances, it's essential to carve out time for your own growth. This applies to everyone, whether you're single with more flexibility or juggling a busy family life. Even those who seem to have "freedom" often struggle with the same issue, saying yes to too many things that don't serve them.

Many people live their lives motivated by guilt. They feel obligated to attend every event, answer every call, or help everyone in crisis. But the truth is, many of these commitments are self-imposed. To better yourself, you need to step back and ask, "Is this really helping anyone? Is this helping me?" You might fear letting people down, but the reality is, the opposite is true. By focusing on your own growth, you become a more vibrant, dynamic person who can offer more to the world, far more than by simply showing up out of obligation.

This shift in perspective allows you to be more intentional with your time and energy. It's not about abandoning people; it's about being clear about what helps you and ultimately, what helps them. Saying "no" when something doesn't align with your growth isn't selfish, it's necessary for creating a more meaningful and productive life.

If your life feels like a mess, it's even more important to focus inward. It's easy to rely on others when things are tough, but you have to take a step back and ask yourself, "How can I help myself?" This might mean slowly, subtly reshaping your life so that it better serves your growth, but it's a critical step.

Start by reframing how you see your obligations. The more you help yourself, the more you're helping the people around you. This might feel counterintuitive at first, but it's the greatest thing you can do to improve the world, make yourself better, and you'll be in a stronger position to help others.

Here's a practical tip. Over the next few days, pay close attention to everything you do. Ask yourself, "Is this helping me grow?" You'll likely discover that a lot of your actions aren't benefiting anyone, they're just habits you've developed, driven by guilt, obligation, or routine.

People often engage in activities that don't serve them. Consider a pity party, for example, people gathering to reinforce their insecurities rather than lifting each other up. Ask yourself, "Is this serving me?" and be honest with the answer. If the answer is no, it's time to start saying no more often.

This isn't easy, and it comes with some consequences. You may need to distance yourself from certain social circles or routines. People may not understand at first, and some might even resist your change. But over time, they'll notice the positive shift in you, and that will speak louder than any explanation.

It's okay to say no. In fact, it's necessary. Sometimes this means turning down invitations or avoiding certain conversations. At other times, it's as simple as not engaging in the usual distractions, whether that's scrolling through social media or spending time in environments that don't support your growth.

Piece by piece, as you start saying no to what doesn't serve you, you'll notice changes. You'll feel better, more focused, and more in control of your life. You'll see that, by prioritizing your own growth, you actually have more energy and space to help others when it truly matters. You'll become a beacon, not just for yourself, but for everyone around you.

YOU ATTRACT WHAT YOU ARE

"A path is only a path, and there is no affront to oneself or to others, in dropping it if that is what your heart tells you." – Carlos Castaneda

You attract what you are. If you want a peaceful life, you must become a peaceful person. If you're after success or wealth, you need to cultivate an abundance mindset. If you're dreaming of the perfect relationship, you must first become the kind of partner capable of building that relationship. One will never come before the other.

Let's break this down practically. This isn't about the law of attraction or discussing energy vibrations. Instead, we'll focus on two concrete things. How the world perceives us and how we view the world around us. Becoming the person you need to be to attract what you want in life is key. When you embody the qualities of the life you desire, you're more likely to see and seize the opportunities that align with those desires.

We've all encountered people who, without saying a word, put us at ease, people with a calm, almost innocent energy that reminds us of simpler times. Then there are the super energetic types, the ones who seem to radiate positivity. After spending time with them, you often walk away feeling a bit of their energy, uplifted and inspired. These people leave a residual impact on you, and their energy influences how you feel and move through the rest of your day.

Why do I bring up these examples? Because they illustrate how intuitive humans are by nature. We all pick up on the subtle energies others project, even before words are exchanged. You can sense calmness, high energy, anger, or peace in others, and they can sense it in you.

Here's the blunt truth, you have to change the way you "smell" (the energy you exude) if you want to attract something different in life. I use this phrase "smell" because it shocks people into understanding that we all give off a certain vibe. Whether it's calmness, trustworthiness, or something else, the world picks up on it. If you want something, whether it's a relationship, job or lifestyle, you need to become the version of yourself who naturally attracts those things.

Take relationships, for example. If you're seeking a fit, active partner, you'll need to become fit and active yourself. It's simple, but often hard work. There are no shortcuts here. If you want to be a CEO, no amount of manifesting will make that happen if you haven't developed the skills, mindset, and habits required to thrive in that role.

It can feel daunting, but it's not impossible. The key is to start small. Identify what you want, then look at who you need to become to get there. This might sound like a massive, life-altering shift, but it doesn't have to be. The process begins by acknowledging that we all have gut instincts, and if you change your energy, even just a little, the way you perceive the world and how the world perceives you will begin to shift.

Once you alter the energy you give off, the rest follows naturally. Your perception of opportunities, people, and situations will begin to change. While it's easy to focus on how others sense your energy, the bigger goal is transforming how you see the world and respond to it. This starts with small, practical changes.

Here's the tip. Pick one thing to change, and you'll see immediate results. It doesn't have to be complicated. Focus on something as simple as your posture, your smile, or how you make eye contact. When I first began my personal growth journey, I found inspiration from a movie character. I admired the way they carried themselves, so I practiced their mannerisms, the way they smiled, said hello, and held themselves in conversation. At first, I felt a bit like a fraud, but over time, those habits became my own.

It's okay to draw inspiration from others, whether it's a fictional character, a family member, or a role model. You weren't born knowing how to shape yourself into the person you want to become. It's a skill you can develop, and you're free to find inspiration wherever you find it.

Start by practicing just one thing, maybe it's your posture, or the way you pause before responding in conversation. Do it for a week, and you'll start to notice the difference. Each small change builds on the next, and over time, these shifts will alter how others perceive you and how you view the world around you. This is how you begin to attract what you want, by becoming the kind of person who naturally draws those things into your life.

It might seem like a lot of work, especially if your goals involve physical effort, like getting in shape. But remember, this is a lifelong journey. You're constantly evolving, and as you change, so will your perception of what's possible for you. Don't get overwhelmed, keep it simple and practical.

If you did this for just a month, if you focused on changing one thing each week, you'd see a significant shift in how you feel, how people interact with you, and the opportunities that present themselves. These changes don't just happen in your mind, they become part of your everyday life.

For those of you further along in your personal growth journey who might feel stuck, my advice is the same, pick one thing and shift it. You already know what you need to do, but sometimes we all get a bit bound up. Start small, even if it's something as basic as your smile or your posture. The momentum will carry you forward.

Ultimately, if you want something in life, you have to become the person capable of receiving it. And that starts by making small, intentional changes. Just pick one thing, practice it, and you'll see results. Your perception will shift, and you'll begin to move toward becoming who you need to be to attract what you desire.

THE WAY YOU DO ONE THING

"Do nothing that is of no use." –
Miyamoto Musashi

"The way you do one thing is the way you do everything." We've all heard this phrase before, but what does it really mean, and how can we apply it in a practical, sustainable way? We often hear these kinds of ideas tossed around, but without a clear sense of how to implement them, they can feel more like motivational fluff than something we can actually use. It took me years to fully grasp this concept, but once I did, it changed everything. When you truly understand it, this idea can transform your life, giving you more energy, focus, and effectiveness in everything you do. And the best part? You'll notice the benefits immediately.

At its core, this concept is about recognizing that when you focus on the small things and do them well, you save energy in the long run. You might have heard the saying, "The easy route is more difficult," or "Cheaper is more expensive." It's all tied to the same idea. Half-measures drain more energy than full efforts because your mind knows when you're cutting corners. The mental load of knowing you didn't give your best depletes you, even when you think you're saving effort.

Let me give you an example I often use with my students, cleaning your house. It's something we all do, and it's an easy way to understand this concept. Most of the time, when we clean, we just pick up the basics, a quick tidy-up that we tell ourselves is "good enough." Every once in a while, we do a deep clean, but typically we coast along with surface-level efforts.

The truth is, your mind knows how thoroughly, or not, you're doing a task, and that knowledge has a direct impact on your energy levels. When you do a job well, your mind rewards you with energy. When you don't, it takes energy from you. Simply doing a task "good enough" doesn't cut it. Your mind is always aware of whether you've truly completed something to the best of your ability, and it will reflect that back to you as either energy gained or energy lost.

Here's a challenge, think about the last time you cleaned the kitchen and did a really thorough job. Didn't you stand back and feel a sense of accomplishment, even energized, despite the effort? Not only do you feel good, but the next time you clean, it's easier because you set a high standard the first time and the bulk of the work is done. It's the difference between "do it right" and "do it twice."

This principle creates a powerful feedback loop. When you approach tasks with intention and give them your best effort, you gain energy, and that energy carries over into the next task. It's a snowball effect. The better you do, the more energy you get, and the more proficient you become.

Building proficiency as a habit starts with small, everyday tasks. We've all met people who seem to have it together, those who are organized, efficient, and always on point. The truth is, you can be that person too, and it begins with how you handle the little things. These habits of excellence start to form when you bring focus to your daily routine, whether it's getting dressed, cleaning up, preparing for work, or even socializing with friends. Many of these things are on autopilot for us, but the goal is to turn off that autopilot and bring mindful attention to everything you do.

Once you start building proficiency into your daily routine, you'll see immediate results. Suddenly, things that felt like chores or obligations become energizing.

The tasks themselves won't be easier or harder, but your approach will change how you experience them.

One of the simplest ways to start is by choosing an area in your living space and doing a deep clean with intention. Commit to it fully. As you get into it, you'll find that you can't stop, there's something about fully engaging with a task that becomes addictive. And when you finish, notice how you feel, accomplished, energized, and ready to tackle the next thing. That energy will propel you forward into the rest of your day.

If you apply this approach to all the small tasks in your life, your energy levels will increase dramatically. It's an immediate turnaround. The more you focus on doing things well, the more energy you'll gain, and over time, this will become second nature. You'll build habits of proficiency that touch every aspect of your life. And the best part? You won't be able to go back to mediocrity, your mind simply won't allow it.

Here's another way you can get started. Choose one small thing and do it with full attention. When you're getting dressed in the morning, focus on putting together your outfit with care. Iron your clothes, take pride in how you groom yourself. Do it as well as you possibly can. After this becomes an automatic routine, choose something else. It could be organizing your desk, planning your day, or preparing a meal. The key is to bring your full attention and effort to each task.

As you continue, these habits will become your new normal. You'll find yourself naturally more focused, more energized, and more proficient in everything you do. People around you will notice, too. You might not be aware of it right away, but others will start to see the difference in your energy, your efficiency, and your overall demeanor.

There's no need for complicated checklists, courses, or motivational speeches. You don't have to rearrange your entire life to get started. Just focus on one thing at a time. Start with something simple, like cleaning an area of your home, and commit to doing it as well as you possibly can. Then move on to the next task with the same intention.

Over time, this approach will transform how you experience your daily life. You'll feel more in control, more productive, and more energized. And as you build these habits, your life will start to align with the kind of person you've always wanted to be, vibrant, proficient, and full of energy.

CORE VALUES

"Awareness is the key to transformation. You must become aware of the agreements and beliefs that are guiding your life in order to change them." – Don Miguel Ruiz Jr.

Understanding your core values is key to understanding who you are, who you want to become, and how to guide your life in the right direction. Most people, however, never take the time to identify their core values, the principles they want to live by. Knowing your core values gives you a clearer sense of self and direction, helping you navigate life's decisions with greater clarity and purpose.

Often, we don't fully understand who we are, let alone who we want to be. And because we haven't taken the time to figure this out, we're left reacting to life rather than actively shaping it. So how do we go about discovering who we are and who we want to become?

One of the best ways to start is by identifying your core values. If you can articulate them, if you can name them on the spot, you'll begin to align your conscious and subconscious mind with the person you want to be. This isn't something we hear about often in a practical way, but it's incredibly powerful. Many of us go through life defining ourselves by external factors, our jobs, our relationships, our backgrounds, without ever digging deeper into what truly matters to us.

To be honest, I don't think most people have given much thought to who they really are or who they want to become. But identifying your core values is a game changer. It shifts your perception and helps you make decisions with more intention. When you know what matters most to you, it influences not only how you see yourself but also how you view the world. It helps you grow because you begin to live in alignment with the person you aspire to be.

Your core values also guide your decision-making process, both big and small. Too often, we're on autopilot, reacting to situations without much thought. But when you've identified your core values, you have a framework for making choices. You can ask yourself, "Does this align with my values?" If it does, great. If not, you know it's not the right path for you. This applies to everyday decisions as well. Your core values start to shape your instincts, and over time, you'll find yourself automatically making decisions that align with them.

This doesn't have to be a complicated or lengthy process. You don't need to spend hour's journaling or go through a formal exercise. Simply taking 15 or 20 minutes to think about your core values is enough to make a significant impact. It will rewire your subconscious mind in ways that will surprise you. When life presents a big decision or opportunity, you can check back in with your values to see if you're still on the right track.

Let's take relationships as an example. I often get questions from students about relationships, and one of the first things I ask is, "How does this fit into your core values?" Whether it's your behavior or the behavior of someone else, how does it align with the principles you've set for yourself? Core values can also serve as aspirations, qualities you want to embody but may not fully have yet. This is important for personal growth. Some people fear they're being inauthentic by aspiring to values they don't yet possess, but this is how we grow. You're not lying to yourself, you're setting a path for who you want to become.

Core values help guide us toward the person we want to be. This is all about self-awareness, taking the time to think about who we are now and who we want to be in the future. And while it may sound like a big undertaking, it doesn't have to be complicated. There are books and manuals out there that break this process down into dozens of steps, but I like to keep it simple.

Here's a practical tip, take 15 minutes to sit down and identify three core values. These values should reflect what's most important to you in how you live your life. They can be simple, like wanting to take care of your loved ones, or being an honest person. Write them down. Even just thinking about them is beneficial, but writing them down makes it real. You'll be surprised how much this shapes your mindset.

If you want to take this a step further, look back at your life and try to identify the values you've been living by up until now. This can help you see where you've been and whether your current values match who you want to become.

One of the reasons I recommend writing down your values is so you can revisit them later. Once you start this process, your mind will naturally return to it, especially when you face challenging or joyful situations. You'll find yourself thinking about your core values more often, which is a great way to stay connected to your goals and personal growth.

Start simple. You don't need to come up with a long list of values right away. Three core values are a great starting point, but you can always expand on them later. When I first did this exercise, I wrote down more than a dozen values. Over time, I realized many of them could be grouped into broader categories. As you grow, your values will evolve too.

For example, one of my core values today is "Be mindful of your perceptions." It's a broad idea that reflects lessons I've learned over decades. This value is both specific and expansive, it reminds me to check my mindset, stay aware of how I view the world, and remain open to growth. It's a mental framework I've built for myself, and it's evolved over time into something deeply personal and meaningful.

As you revisit your core values, you'll see how they shift with your personal growth. At first, they might be highly specific, but over time, they'll condense into broader, more meaningful principles. For me, this evolution reflects growth, and it's a sign that my values have become more integrated into my life.

In the early stages of my personal growth, I would intentionally revisit my core values, checking in to see how they were shaping my decisions and actions. Now, it happens naturally. As I encounter new ideas or experiences, I adjust my values to reflect my current understanding of who I am and who I want to be. Over time, my values have become less specific and more about overarching ideas.

Core values are not only a tool for self-awareness, they're a tool for growth. They help us see who we are, who we want to become, and how we want to live our lives. By taking the time to identify your values, you create a foundation for personal growth and a guide for how to navigate life's challenges and opportunities.

THE MAP & THE TERRITORY

"The voyage of discovery is not in seeking new landscapes but in having new eyes." – Marcel Proust

The world is vast, dynamic, and full of opportunity. Whether you're seeking career success, a fulfilling relationship, launching a business, or simply striving for a peaceful life, everything you want is out there, waiting for you. The challenge, though, lies in perception. Our personal view of the world, our own personal bubble can limit us. This chapter will explore how our perception may be trapping us and how we can shift it to recognize and seize opportunities that are often right in front of us.

More often than not, what holds us back isn't a lack of opportunity, but our limited perspective. We tend to search for what we want only within our immediate surroundings or our familiar ways of thinking. But the truth is, the world is a fluid, ever-changing place, and there are countless situations and people that can help make your dreams a reality. If we remove concepts like manifestation and look at it purely from a mathematical standpoint, the ideal circumstances or connections for whatever you desire already exist. The problem is that we haven't yet put ourselves in a position to take advantage of them. Sometimes, we don't even recognize opportunities when they're right in front of us.

The core issue is that we often look for solutions, relationships, or opportunities based on what we already know. We stay within our own personal sphere, our learned perception, without challenging it. The world is enormous, and though it's impossible to see everything, the perfect scenario for what you want is out there. That much, I can guarantee.

Embracing this idea requires a shift in mindset. Once you start to push beyond your usual way of seeing things, your mind will gradually begin to notice the opportunities around you. But here's the tricky part, this realization comes after you've made the shift. You have to begin the process first. You have to be willing to break out of your usual patterns of thinking, to "snap out of it," as I like to say, and only then will your perception start to change.

I still struggle with this at times, even after years of personal growth work. It's not easy to break free from your personal bubble. But once you do, you'll start to see opportunities that were always there but hidden from your previous view.

To illustrate, think about the experience of buying a new car. Suddenly, it feels like you see that same car everywhere. Those cars were always there; it's just that your perception has shifted, and now you're noticing them. A similar thing happened to me once while hat shopping. I was on the hunt for a classic 1950s fedora, like the ones in old detective noir films. After spending a day in upscale hat shops, my friend and I left to get lunch. As we walked, we started noticing people wearing hats all over the place. My friend commented on this, my reply was simple, "The hats were always there." Our perception had simply tuned in to what we wanted to see.

This is how perception works, it is proof that we see what we're primed to see. Our mental filters can limit us. But the good news is, we can actively challenge these filters and train ourselves to see the world in new ways.

So, how do we challenge our perceptions and open our minds to opportunities we might otherwise miss? The first step is to "snap out of it." You need to disrupt your routine, shake up your perspective, and steer your mind in a new direction. One of the simplest ways to do this is by attending events you wouldn't normally go to, something outside your comfort zone.

At least once a year, I make a point of attending an event I wouldn't usually be interested in. For me, this could be the opera or a completely random show. The reason I do this is to jolt myself out of my usual patterns. When I immerse myself in something unfamiliar, I'm suddenly surrounded by people who are deeply passionate about it, and I get a glimpse into a culture or lifestyle I wouldn't normally encounter. It challenges my perceptions and opens me up to new ideas and possibilities.

I also make a habit of going to social events regularly, often picking them at random. You never know who you'll meet or what fresh perspective you'll gain. Even if you're feeling anti-social, attending a gallery or exposition can serve the same purpose, exposing you to new ideas and creative energy. This is especially useful if you have a specific goal or idea in mind. Target events or activities that are outside your usual sphere but loosely related to what you're pursuing.

If you're stuck in the same routine with the same group of friends, you're not challenging your perception.

You're staying within your bubble. The key is to put yourself in situations that push you beyond your usual experiences. If there was an opportunity within your current sphere, you would have already found it. By stepping out of your comfort zone, you start to see the world from a broader perspective, and that's when new opportunities present themselves.

It's important to remember that this process doesn't have to be complicated. If you're introverted or hesitant about attending social events, start small. Go to a public exposition or gallery. Observe what others are doing, especially those who are motivated and passionate about their work. It can be humbling to see how much is happening in the world outside your bubble. You'll begin to realize just how much potential is out there for you, too.

If you live in a smaller town or rural area, this might mean driving into a larger city for events. Do it. It's always worth it. While you can explore online, nothing beats the tangible experience of meeting people and seeing the world with your own eyes.

There's also the idea of manifestation, which I've come to believe in after years of experience. The universe is creative by nature, and life wants to give you what you desire. If you stop and think about it, life has already given you exactly what you've focused on up to this point. The trick is learning how to shift your perception to see and seize the opportunities that align with your goals.

You have to trust in the vastness of the world and your own ability to connect with it. But this won't happen unless you put yourself out there and challenge your perception. Once you do, opportunities will begin to reveal themselves.

The simplest and most effective way to start is by attending new events and talking to new people. This shakes up your perception and puts you in a position to see opportunities that were always there but hidden from your previous view.

Most people can't see the opportunities in front of them, even when they're clearly presented. People can be handed an opportunity on a silver platter and not even see it. This might sound harsh, but it's true. I've seen it time and again. Our limited frame of reference blinds us to the possibilities. But if you make even a small effort to shift your perception, you'll start to notice things you never saw before.

If you want to get the most out of life and achieve your dreams, you must step beyond your personal bubble and shift your perception. Once you start, the momentum builds. You'll see opportunities that were always there but just outside your line of sight. And with this new perspective, the world opens up in ways you never imagined.

THE WORLD IS A MIRROR

"We do not see things as they are, we see them as we are." – Anaïs Nin

Everything in life, our experiences, successes, problems, even the drama we encounter, is directly shaped by our perception. The way we view the world influences the quality of our life, the jobs we hold, the relationships we have, and the opportunities we see or miss. If we want to improve our lives, one of the most important things we can do is train ourselves to have healthy, realistic perceptions. In this chapter, we'll explore how perception and projection shape our reality, how to manage them, and why it's essential to take control of these processes.

Seeing reality as it truly is, both in the world around us and within ourselves, is a critical skill. But it's not enough just to aim for clarity; we should also train our perception to incorporate positivity. Why? Because how we see the world not only affects our actions and moods but also determines the opportunities we recognize. Training your perception to see things accurately while also leaning toward the positive is one of the most impactful ways to improve your life.

Cultivating critical thinking starts with managing your perception and projections. Without this foundation, our ability to think critically, recognize opportunities, and attract what we want in life will always be hindered. Things will remain skewed, and progress will feel out of reach. But once you train your mind to see clearly, everything changes.

One of the greatest benefits of managing our perception is the ability to see motives, both in ourselves and others. When you can strip away the layers of assumption and bias, you gain the ability to understand what's really going on in any given situation. You start asking essential questions: What is this person's true intention? Where are they coming from? What's my own state of mind? What's really going on here?

Another key advantage is self-protection. By sharpening your perception, you become more intuitive, allowing you to avoid people or situations that might cause harm. At the same time, this skill enables you to attract positive, like-minded people who encourage and uplift you.

In life, one of the most important things, second only to self-awareness, is the ability to attract what you want. But here's the catch, you can't attract what you can't see. I often talk about the importance of recognizing opportunities, and I can't stress it enough. Many people desire opportunities, but they wouldn't be able to see one even if it was right in front of them. Our perception and projections are key to unlocking these opportunities.

In its simplest form, our perception colors everything we experience. You could be in a conversation with someone, making assumptions about them or their intentions, and those assumptions might be completely wrong. This happens when our projections, unchecked, take over and create a false reality based on our own biases or desires. We think we're seeing the truth, but we're often mistaken.

Take, for example, someone who is perpetually angry. Their worldview is filled with negativity and conflict. In every situation, they see only problems and hostility, but that doesn't mean the situation is inherently negative. It's simply what they're projecting onto it. We must be very cautious of these types of thought patterns.

The world reflects back who we are. Every situation we encounter mirrors our internal state. This is why managing perception and projection is so crucial, they shape the reality we experience.

One way I started gaining control over this years ago was by practicing with everyday situations. I'd take simple, mundane moments, like standing in line at the grocery store or sitting in traffic, and try to view them from different angles. I'd imagine the people around me having various emotions: maybe that person is happy, maybe they're having a rough day. The idea is to force yourself to see situations from multiple perspectives, even when they seem routine.

Another practical example is dealing with traffic. When someone cuts you off or speeds past, instead of immediately reacting with frustration, try imagining different reasons for their behavior. Perhaps they're in a rush because of an emergency, or maybe they're simply distracted by a good day. The point is to challenge your initial reaction by considering other possibilities.

Managing your perceptions and projections takes time and effort, it's one of the most challenging yet rewarding things you can do for yourself. Without this skill, you may not be seeing the reality of the situations around you, which means you're missing out on countless opportunities.

Many of us go through life believing we understand what's happening in any given situation, but more often than not, we're wrong. Once you start shifting your perception and viewing situations from different angles, you'll begin to see the truth of what's really going on, both with other people and within yourself. You'll realize how much your preconceptions and automatic thought patterns have shaped your experience of the world.

The key is to start somewhere. It can be tough to manage your internal perceptions right away, so I recommend starting by practicing outwardly in the world. Look at everyday situations and consciously try to see them from different angles. Your mind will gradually get used to this exercise, and over time, it will start applying the same flexibility to your inner world.

Once you've built this skill, sprinkle a bit of positivity into your perceptions. One of the simplest ways to do this is by giving people the benefit of the doubt. Seeming faults in our perception are often most obvious when we see something negative. When you encounter what you perceive to be a negative situation, try giving everyone involved, including yourself, the benefit of the doubt. This approach shifts your mind and allows you to see things from different viewpoints more easily.

In time, your mind will become adept at distinguishing between what's coming from inside you and what's truly happening outside. You'll be able to come closer to the truth of situations, not just your version of it. And remember, as you embark on this journey, the truth is subjective. There's no single "truth" out there waiting to be uncovered, but by managing your perceptions, you can get closer to a clearer, more empowering view of the world.

NOTES

NOTES

NOTES

NOTES

NOTES

NOTES

www.ingramcontent.com/pod-product-compliance
Lightning Source LLC
Chambersburg PA
CBHW020332130626
46549CB00003B/1145